ABOUT THE DEAD

May Swenson
Poetry Award Series
Volume 15

ABOUT THE DEAD

poems
by

Travis Mossotti

UTAH STATE UNIVERSITY PRESS
Logan, Utah
2011

Utah State University Press
Logan, Utah 84322-3078

Publication credits appear in the acknowledgments.
Manufactured in the United States of America.

Cover art "St. Francis Contemplating a Skull" by Josh Mossotti.
Original interior artwork by Josh Mossotti.
Cover series design by Barbara Yale-Read.

ISBN 9780874218268 (cloth)
ISBN 9780874218275 (paper)
ISBN 9780874218282 (ebook)

Library of Congress Cataloging-in-Publication Data

Mossotti, Travis.
  About the dead / Travis Mossotti.
    p. cm. — (May Swenson poetry award series ; v. 15)
    ISBN 978-0-87421-826-8 (cloth) — ISBN 978-0-87421-827-5 (pbk.) — ISBN 978-0-87421-828-2 (e-book)
  I. Title.
  PS3613.O788A64 2011
  811'.6—dc22
                          2011018018

For
Family and Friends

CONTENTS

Judging the May Swenson Poetry Competition is a fine way to make yourself a hundred enemies—poets who cut off a slice of their heart and handed it to you in an envelope and you looked at it, nodded, turned away—but that's just how life is and that's why we guard our hearts. May Swenson guarded hers. She wrote beautiful descriptive poems about bronco riding, the Museum of Modern Art, and the A train (the same train that Duke Ellington took), but she was guarded about her fleeing Utah for New York City, and she had her reasons.

I was invited to judge the contest, I suppose, because, like most readers, I am exasperated by so much poetry I read and exhilarated by some, and my reactions have little to do with schools or styles. Books of poetry with bewildering blurbs on the back ("she shows an eclectic intelligence combined with forensic lyricism and digressive intensity")—and you plow through a few poems and they are so unrewarding:

Spilled perfections linger
Near the legendary lipstick blinking
As she chews the burrito
    Of anonymity.

And you say, "Oh give me a break," and the next book is *Blurred Undulations of Fevered Sobriety* ("compellingly intense with an almost rapturous phenomenology") and the first poem begins:

How perfect the spillage of burrito
    On your lipstick. I blink.
You don't know me.
    How convenient.

And so it goes.

Travis Mossotti's *About the Dead* struck me on first reading as an adventurous book grounded in real places and real people, and reading it was like following the poet up a steep climb on a rocky slope as he improvised his route, and at every step I was struck by the rightness of his choices, surprised by so many odd words that seemed so *exactly right*. It's not a slope I would ever climb myself, not language I would use, which makes the book astonishing, lively, fresh and worth repeated reading. The drunken boys in "Decampment" leaving the quarry—

A train of empty boxcars slugged by before dawn
and carried us back to Aynor like kings

defeated.

The dream about the girl Grace—"I wanted to open her like a mason
jar / from the cellar hold." The contrition for having paid Marcy $50
to have sex with him and his friend.

Forgive me,

when she pulled me under the sheets
Her eyes went somewhere else. Outside,

the heat lightning kept drawing
its thread across the horizon.

And then:

Our house sank two inches
the day after my father died.

I could, if forced at gunpoint, write a decent term paper about Mr.
Mossotti's book—I really could—and get into the gender trajectories
of interbeing, but I am older now and what I am grateful for is the
simple pleasure of narrative by a writer inspired to take chances. So
when I read,

Try asking Ernie Watts, a local bricklayer,
to explain how after a long day of work
and league night at the Lucky Strike
he can glide across the kitchen floor,
Old Style hovering like a ghost on his breath,
bowling shoes slung over one shoulder,
singing *fly me to the moon* to his wife Cheryl.

I am in a real kitchen, tuned in to a beautiful story I think I already
know, all the way to the blessed thump of the last line: "there is no
other life but this."

The dead armadillos; the spirit of the trucker left behind in the
walls of the Red Roof Inn; the boxcar riding through the country

of forgotten languages; the locust waving to the man looking for his keys; the wild perfection of "Getting Arrested" ("I know I'm not the only drunk in the tank"); Angela dancing with her castanets while Henry is "humming whiskey / through a harmonica"; the ghost frying chicken in a cast iron skillet; Van Gogh searching for the right shade of yellow; the little gator toothing open his shell. The becoming humility of "Float Trip" about the poet and his fellow writers and artists going to Sullivan, Missouri, to float on inner tubes down the Meramec River—

> weekend philosophers bent on solidifying
> our contempt for the local stock whose
>
> imagination carries them back to a leather
> sofa in the den and a NASCAR Sunday . . .
>
> I apologize for our unwelcome intrusion.
> We offer nothing; we take it all in return.

And now I'll stop quoting from Mr. Mossotti's book and let you read it for yourself and follow him up the rock face. He offers good value in return, a hard-earned climb to a magnificent view.

Garrison Keillor

I thought only to study live things, thought
never to know so much about the dead.

Natasha Trethewey
Native Guard

ABOUT THE DEAD

DECAMPMENT

-Aynor, SC

I.

Long before the night my father and I hiked the rim
of chicory and sedge that marked our property,
generations of ghosts already meandered down
the ephemeral streambeds' smoothed cavities,
making camp under colonies of black elm, cypress.

We built a fire, and he told me stories: Kiawah,
runaway slaves, Confederate or Union soldiers
passing through—this year cotton, last year tobacco,
lockjaw, gadfly sores, goat milk souring, bone shank
in the horse trough. His great-grandfather
Edmund gave cornmeal, blankets, tourniquets,

board or passage without question,
let them rest awhile on his land,
on this soil full of ache: bleeding, giving birth.

Twelve years old, burning daylight,
I waited for my mother's dinner call
to scurry the quail from the fencerows.

I kicked loose rocks in the dirt,
hoped I'd find arrowheads,
bullets or links of iron,
gray as leaf-fire fading into a storm.

This was where I first discovered
exactly what this land was missing.

II.

The first night I thought a woman
was getting raped, but by the third
my father had me holding the light
while he loaded buckshot.

A screech owl had made its home
in the magnolia near the work shed—
my mother and sister Cora, waiting
inside, listened to Beethoven's

Moonlight Sonata on the record player.
Together, we stalked, patient
for rustle or twitch to set our aim.

Ten minutes passed, we figured
it was done for the night and turned back
toward the house, relieved of duty—

then, inches over our heads,
quiet as laundry gusting on the line,
the owl flew past. My father didn't blink,

didn't shoot. *Must've been a ghost leaving*, he said.

III.

Mr. Jacobs, the deacon at church, taught me prayers
to say before bed, blessings for the meatloaf,
mashed potatoes, fried okra, and sweet bread.
One year I prayed for rain every night just to see
if it would take, but a dry wind set over us,
drier than bone dust. I prayed the opposite,
and it only got worse; at church, my father
overheard the Kissee family whispering.

During the night they packed up and left.

Then the other prayers started. Each night:
a field of red-winged blackbirds on fire,
canker sores for the Pearson dogs,
gadflies, thick and dark as molasses,
sweeping Aynor off the map in a black rush.

It became enough to watch them in my head,
to see the lame mule sent to the guillotine
and wake up without deference to the sun.

IV.

My father signed over the eastern swathes of land
to gird the lien; Colin Pearson and I stole
a bottle of whiskey from the diesel-plex
glimmering near the off-ramp.

Both of us were stupid drunk by the time
we made it to the quarry and built
a bonfire on the ledge.
The moon in the pool below shattered

with curses, with stones, with showers of embers.
A train of empty boxcars slugged by before dawn
and carried us back to Aynor like kings

defeated. I threw up three times in a ditch,
dunked my head into a bucket of rainwater,

stepped inside, a new man.

V.

Overripe, I tumbled to the orchard floor.

Mrs. Jacobs gathered me up with her apron,
left me on the sill cooling all afternoon.

Brother elm was kindling a fire.

My father had brought the good axe.

I dreamed the night swallowed us down
      its rough tongue.

Grace Kissee walking under a row of hackberry
made me ache.

I wanted to open her like a mason jar
from the cellar hold—

                apple sluice,
            red wolf howl avalanching
            the valley's winter gourd,
            petroglyphs, folktales,
            blue skies complicated with clouds.

I dreamed a sharp knife with no leather.

      I dreamed black longings from the bluffs.

I dreamed the sweet flag urged me knee-deep
      into the stream.

VI.

Forgive the girl, it wasn't her fault.
Hitching three days with rotten luck,

all she wanted was enough money
for a motel room and a bus ticket west.

Forgive the earth for not swallowing
Colin and me and his truck and our deal

for her, for Marcy, for the hot shower,
for the clean clothes, for the fifty dollars

we promised after she finished
with both of us. Forgive me,

when she pulled me under the sheets
her eyes went somewhere else. Outside,

the heat lightning kept drawing
its thread across the horizon.

VII.

Our house sank two inches
the day after my father died.

The foundation split. My mother
kept tripping over the new cracks
in the front porch, and Cora
spun a screwdriver on the rail.
My head filled with cement.
That night, I hiked four miles

over rotting trestle
to the abandoned quarry,

shallow limestone awning,
twigfire, two drifters turning
skewered rabbits over the flame.
One of them scooted a burlap sack,
asked, *You lost, son?*

ONE

Country of Forgotten Languages

INSIDE THE SKULL

-after a painting by Francisco de Zurbarán

Once inside the skull, I felt free to choose the décor
without recourse or disapproval, so I hung a portrait
of myself on the western cranial wall, potted two

African violets and placed them on an end table
(two inspires competition for light and affection).

I rolled out my grandmother's Slovakian rug,
and upon it, two folding chairs facing
the ocular windows. Soon enough,

morning came stampeding into the room
like someone had opened a blast-furnace door.

Venetian blinds crossed my mind. I just thought
of the words, and there they were,
a flood of orange gathering at my feet.

From then on, willing things into existence
occupied my time: first, I was bitter, gorgeous,

chiseled from marble, and then on the eastern wall
a mirror appeared; second, she appeared: I named her
Darla. I conjured a decanter, Cornish hens, a kitchen table.

That night, I invented a bed where we made love. The next
morning the folding chairs were replaced with a couch

I must've dreamed up, with Darla on it, resting.
She said, *It was like it just occurred to me*, rubbing a hand
over her rounded and very pregnant stomach.

Out the window, I noticed a mendicant dressed in rags,
edging closer to us along an old goat-herder's path

under a variegated row of stone pine. He lifted us up,
cradled us in his palms like we were a strange
and fragile object—peered with the intensity

of a man walking through a darkened field. But soon,
his eyes dropped to the ground like a broken mule,

like someone who understands he's been cheated.
It's as if he had seen something that wasn't there.
It's as if he had seen us cowering inside.

CROSSING THE GAP

Try asking Ernie Watts, a local bricklayer,
to explain how after a long day of work
and league night at the Lucky Strike
he can glide across the kitchen floor,
Old Style hovering like a ghost on his breath,
bowling shoes slung over one shoulder,
singing *fly me to the moon* to his wife Cheryl.
And when he dips her over the linoleum
like it was their first homecoming all over again,
ask him to put into words what that sinking is,
that shudder in his chest, as he notices
the wrinkles gathering at the corners of her mouth.
He'd rather tell you about the time they rode
the Tail of the Dragon the year after they'd married,
crossing Deals Gap at the Tennessee state line
on his '77 Triumph Silver Jubilee.
How they heard talk of a young couple
dying on that same stretch of road a week before,
and how hard she held onto him that day—
curve after potentially deadly curve.
Afterwards, in bed, she'll reach for the Virginia Slims
on the nightstand, and he'll open
the windows behind the headboard
as a summer breeze creeps past the lithesome curtains—
wild grass and honeysuckle mixing with the tobacco.
If the drone and flicker of a gathering storm should disrupt
the silence of the room, she'll tighten the wing nut
of her body behind his, so close that when her lips
brush against the nearly imperceptible hairs
on the back of his neck he'll be convinced
there is no other life but this.

PEREGRINATION

In recent
history,
the plated
armadillo
became
determined
to travel
northward
to Illinois
and beyond.
I know of this
journey
only from
sad little
remains
on shoulders
of highways,
from windows
of speeding
automobiles,
from darkened
crests of blue
mountains.

RED ROOF INN

I.

The mattress had a dead-man's
give to it. I snapped off
a rabbit ear, set it on the table.

I had the place to myself.

Nobody fucked on the other side
of the wall unless they fucked
like a breezeway door,
like a five-minute shower.

I left my boots on the mat.
I paid cash for everything.

I wanted you
to find me like this.
That would've meant something.

Instead, blind static,
room reeking from the awful,
yellow liver of the last trucker
who slept here. He must've still been
in the walls, part of him at least:
a work flannel, a pair of boots
tossed aside.

Dark enough, early morning,
I bit the end off my last cigar,
fired it up like a cat's eye.

No way would the fog keep me
from leaving.

II.

You never believed me when I said
I didn't have the guts to kill him:

dark guts, blackwatch guts,
sawdust-burning-quick guts.

He squirmed
in pig shit,

blood rose
in his throat,

Death's knees on his chest.

One time, and it carved me up inside.

One lousy time and you swore it meant nothing,
kept kissing my hands
like I was a goddamned saint.

I snatched the shotgun from the shelf.
I left myself.
It happened that easy.

ALICE

Walking down the highway's soft shoulder
on the way to you, I passed a single lichen
covered boulder the color of your eyes.
I brushed it with the backs of my fingers
half-believing you watched from the pines
like an owl. A quarter-moon stalked
from a distance, and I imagined you, alone,
standing in a doorframe, wrapped in a quilt,
cigarette lazing between your fingers.
Maybe it was the seam of your black stocking
I trailed through Appalachia, chicken dinner
cooling on a billboard, the sky opening up
its empty skull, gravel dust powdering
my unkempt hair with the same dull ivory
of the letter you sent telling me not to come,
for the sake of your children who by then
were bean stalks winding their way up your legs.
Half the state of Tennessee still lay between us.
I unrolled my sleeping bag on top of a flattened
patch of thistle and saw grass near the trees
and dreamed I was riding a boxcar through
a country of forgotten languages—a field
of cotton on the verge of telling me a secret.

I'M EXPLAINING A FEW THINGS

There's an old bullet lodged in the field of scrub
behind my house that's grown colorless as dirt.

The land is implacable, even as its familiar scene
of death and light retreats into the browning dusk.

Offspring of the offspring of the offspring
of crows cross over the thistle and brush,

cross over ground that remembers nothing of human loss.

STILL-LIFE MINUS FRUIT

Morning rolls over on its side
as delicately as an African violet
first unfurls petals of pink and
white, and you are still a thousand
miles away, asleep; your dreams
puncturing the walls of incalculable
distances. You will scribble down
your dim reflections on the skein
of water pouring from the showerhead
and consider the simple pleasure
of warmth laved over your nipples—
my lips traveling against all odds
and practicality to meet them.

THE DEAD CAUSE

On the porch, a grasshopper waved
its serrated foreleg at me while I juggled

groceries for keys; it was the kind
of friendly wave I might've expected

from a loved one, recently dead,
reincarnated into this green husk.

The whole ordeal triggered an alarm
of distant thunder, stuffing my head

with dark seeds; so after waving back,
I ducked inside, fearful

of inadvertently giving the dead cause
to haunt me—the last thing

I needed. Regina was off doing research
in Glen Rose again, otherwise

she would've identified the grasshopper
using the scientific precision that always

fussed my mouth with cobwebs.
As it was, I dialed her number

just to make sure she was okay,
that she wasn't yet a grasshopper.

Probably nothing more than a locust—Melanoplus
spretus, she said. *It could've been Buddha. Maybe*

I should've invited it in for tea, I said before saying
goodbye. Raindrops the size of doorknobs

began chasing a garbage truck past
the kitchen window. I set the kettle

on the stove to boil, and with curtains
curled back slightly, watched a procession

of locusts lope out from the tall grass,
apparently no longer waiting for an invitation.

HENRY'S BLUES

My musician neighbor hollows out
a piece of sky with his guitar,
until there's room left
for nobody but him—
a broken concerto

he still lugs around
for Angela, his ex-wife,
each chord fouling
in the attic of his chest.
I watched them once,

through the window: Angela
pinched her little castanets
like lotus blossoms,
and danced slow twirls
around the kitchen table;

Henry, humming whiskey
through a harmonica, blessed
her sweet can with a spatula,
while night's ivory sullied
outside. That dim memory

keeps me listening past dark,
listening till there's no music left,
till the only recognizable sound
is the canter of railcars passing
through the nearby train yard.

PASSPORT

Like terminal cases, my eyes
slouch the dim corridors of 3 A.M.,
revisiting the shepherd's cabin

in the French Alps where twilight
smoothed to cinder and I imagined
rounded hills rose in the bedroom

only to find your profile backlit
by a fireplace—all night
that night we wore each other

like old hangers in new clothes.

PREPARING THE TABLE

Robert slouched
over his family's
cast-iron skillet
preparing
fried chicken,
back
to the table,
free hand
tending
to a Barclay.
Nothing felt
the least bit
out of place
until it occurred
to me that we'd
buried Robert
last spring:
everyone
in funeral attire,
prayer hands
conducting
little vigils
in the pews . . .
I was certain
of this much.
Robert counted
heads around
the kitchen table,
and when
we'd finished eating,
he sent us home
with leftovers.

AT CHURCH

At the Sixth Street
Baptist Church

a poor woman
kneels, rubs beads,

trades her sack
of magic beans

back for the cow,
wonders if God

sometimes
mistakenly

visits earth
with open arms

in the form
of tidal waves.

OUTSIDE PINCKNEYVILLE

the great hydraulic claw of a machine
tears up a railroad line fallen to disuse

and overwhelmed with scrub growth
along the highway's rural path. An

enormous animal once drifted to sleep
and died—each heft of scrapwood,

another vertebra loosed from its long
and elegant spine.

WHEAT FIELD WITH CROWS

In the end, a pair of blackbirds took control
of the woodpecker nest and the dead birch tree
in our backyard. Late morning, and the sprig

of sunlight on the breakfast table has turned
into a pale flood of sulfur. I duck barefoot
with toast and black coffee past our bedroom

where you still sleep, to my desk, my notebook
with yesterday's notes: *much of nature is unnerving,*
the twilight rut, the sunrise over the spoiled harvest.

Van Gogh would wake at his house in Arles,
just as the sower left for the field. He spent
entire days under the blazing Provençal sun

until he hit a *high yellow note—yellow, pale lemon, gold.*
How beautiful yellow is, draped over the peat bogs
of Drenthe, or the rooftops in Saintes-Maries de la Mer.

Now, somewhere outside my office window I hear
the ousted woodpecker foraging like a typewriter,
trying to get at some kind of larva just under the wood.

TWO
About the Dead

CREATING THE GARDEN

Here, we have a fountain with a waterfall,
and all around us a chorus of bees
feasts on purple blossoms
that hang from the fingers
of ivy sprawled
like a jester's hat
across the wrought-iron gate.
It is as though this scene,
so festooned in morning sun,
was expelled from the body
of Garden: an exorcism,
or perhaps an adenoma
lumped and bloodied
in a sterilized dish.
Along the path,
the loosed petals
have turned gray as ash
and ought to be swept
from the cobblestones.
But for now, we'll sit together
and listen to the lithesome friction
of the fountain spilling
water into a basin of water.

THE SECOND COMING OF CHRIST IN THE FORM OF A NORTH AMERICAN ALLIGATOR

Somewhere amidst the reclaimed wetlands
between Naples and Ft. Lauderdale,

a little gator tooths open his shell, crawls
out of the womb of mud and stillborn brothers

into his mother's mouth and is led directly
to water. Nearby a man in khaki shorts—

elastic sewn into the waistband, top shirt
buttons undone—remains oblivious

to everything but a rusted lug nut. Time
and again he pauses to wipe the sweat

from his neck with a kerchief, but fails
to feel the ground waxing holy beneath him,

fails to recognize this new Bethlehem
born in a bed of sweet flag and standing water,

this hatchling, sizing things up, tastes the residue
of the after and before world still in the air.

TODAY, HOUDINI IS BURIED

A dime museum sideshow, a circus Wild Man—
Houdini is man. Houdini's brain has become
brain candy for grubs that burst and surge
and well up from the soil when it rains.
Houdini is straightjacketed in this poem,
strung from his ankles, locked in a tank,
starring in a movie, burning up at the Garrick,
mortally crying for somebody to do something—
let him out, or let him die, cause either way
he's grown tired of this place. Houdini in
an oversized milk can is more show than man.
Houdini softly dying in a hospital bed with a leaky
appendix is spot on. Houdini's dying breath?
Just another escape gone off as planned. Today,
Houdini is buried—fresh soil heaped on his grave.
Next spring's grass will cover the brown earth.
A thousand years of wind will weather his name
from our memory. Houdini is God! Houdini
is man bound in chains eyeing the exits.

FUNHOUSE OF MIRTH

I don't want realism, I want magic! Yes, yes, magic!
I try to give that to people.

~Blanche DuBois
A Streetcar Named Desire

I just can't prop up another listless sap in an overcoat,
walking between the tenement's late rows, bending down

to tie his shoe, tipsy, cheap whiskey fogging his breath,
a comet exploding on the street. Who knows, who cares

if he's got ducks in a row or an upside-down mortgage?
It should be enough I pay taxes and mind my peace

while the streetcar hustlers rattle off their linear aphorisms
all the livelong June: like, *when it rains it pours cats and dogs,*

or, *you gotta get up pretty early to turn a sleeping whore
into a saint.* If there's a storyline here it spirals

like a tourniquet and only has room for two strangers
waving pistols from the Pyrenees to a truck stop waitress

in Kansas. They can dance with Siamese twins civilly,
but if you want to know how to solve today's Jumble

bother someone else—cream-cheese glyphs
with a Morse-code baseline, and now you're speaking

their language. Take off your shoes, please. This house
isn't much to look at, but things here can turn on a dime.

BOX

Olive pit, cheese cube, salt on a blanket.
I opened the wine, cranked the box,

and you fumbled out on a spring,
one breast larger than a Japanese pear,

a cannonball for sky. *Oligarchies,*
you said, pointing to Orion's belt,

require a tremendous amount of faith
from us plebeians in order to function.

Meteors started blackjacking over
the horse farm—six years old again,

baby tooth dangling from its nerve.
I worked it all day like a porch swing,

finally broke down and told my mother.
She plucked it on the count of three.

I don't know why I thought of that.
If God has such big plans for us all,

why keep them buried in a fish tank
treasure chest? Why not hand them

out in the soup-lines, you said.
I didn't know. I listened to peepers,

a horse creeping up to the fencepost.
I guess I'm just not very sentimental, I said.

Why is someone trying to play my head
like an accordion again? God's angels,
Charlie's angels? If my eyes were rifles,

I'd have to be softer with my sharp glances
and daggered eyes and orgasm eyes that go
all the way through bed frame, carpet, and

subterranean mole caves to the liquid stuff
at the core where God races chariots and
Satan waits with his infernal bone to pick.

This isn't a confession. But when asked
to say grace over the turkey and gravy boat
at my in-laws, it came out, *Forgive me, Father,*

for I have sinned, and a TV war still lingered
in the living room, but it's hard to care
when there's always more pay-per-view

porn. America, I have the solution if things
get a little boring. One of us has to die.
The other simply pulls the trigger.

VARIATIONS ON A POLITICAL THEME

I.

Stop picking pennies off the ground!
You're making us all look discontent.

II.

There was a time when you'd slice up
the whole watermelon,
invite us neighbors over
for a little music,
run a flag up the pole, call
the meeting into session.

Now your socks can't get white enough.
Now your bread tastes like sulfur
and the potatoes won't grow.

III.

I pledge my faith to the glass chapel,
to fire my rifle like a man.

My loyalty goes to the highest bidder,
and my allegiance to sky earth city country god,
in that order.

Neighbor, you've never established perimeters.
Go help the others sew patches to our uniforms.
I'll cordon us off with razor wire.
I'll boil the hambone myself.

AN APOLOGY

Spiritual enlightenment is nothing more than a card trick
called fifty-two-card-pick-up, and those dumptruck lights
beaming down on you, that's death, and

in the afterlife you get a home movie
about your life: the birth scene, the bicycle scene,
the groping for the clasp of your first C-cup scene.

You watch it the way an ascetic watches a leaf.
There are no interruptions from global warming.
No delivery guy knocks on the door asking you

to please sign for your neighbor's oxygen tanks.
Remember him? Wheezing down the driveway
to the mailbox and back up in just under an hour;

probably one of those poor suckers Monsanto
tried to bury in asbestos—but wait a minute,
this is your afterlife, the one you paid for,

the one you sat on your hands your entire life for,
ignoring every vengeful, lustful, and hateful impulse for.
You know what, I hate people like you. Pretending to be

so sanctimonious when clearly you'd like nothing more
than to carpet-bomb the stinking lot of yahoos and
redneck gurus and corporate litigates and buglers

and wasters and speakeasy filchers and free market
degenerates who gambled away your father's retirement,
yanking the ripcords on their golden parachutes.

Maybe your time down here might've been better spent
learning to fire an M-16 instead of patchworking daisies
into your coffin lining. I apologize, that last one was out of line.

SAXIFRAGE

The gym's boxing room has the sunken décor
of a Fifties bomb shelter—a heavy bag
girthier than an elephant's penis, loafing
pendulumatic long after the barrage of punches
have stopped. I used to imagine pummeling

the chops of the guy who slept with my ex.
Thump, Wham! Thump, Thump, Wham!
Knucklebone. Catharsis. Wingèd prayer
field-dressed like a pheasant. But sooner
or later, everyone has to move on: tornado

swipples a huddle of yearlings from the field,
event horizon of the astrophysicist's wet dream,
ice-cream truck caterwauling over a cliff,
karma mule-kicking the dimwit wiping dust
from the dictator's silly fresco. *Thump, Thump,*

Thump, Thump, Wham! Thump, Wham!
How useful would all the hitting actually be
at say, fending off a grizzly bear? Blitzkrieg?
Ice age? Fists already chafing rosily. Sweat
bilging the usual spots. Sweet grass, duckweed

tupelo, box wood, juniper, box wood, juniper,
flotillas of swamp sunflowers! Quickly now!
Fasten the heroic couplets to stone tablets.
Help me etch the stupid past into the future. *Thump,*
Wham! Thump, Wham! Wham! Florida's not just

for the elderly anymore. Picasso. Latrine. Homunculus.
Filch. And as for the guy that slept with my ex, I never
moved on; he's still my flower that splits the rock—
each punch ratcheted squarely into a pit
of black canvas, my all-purpose jackstraw.

BARBER

Such sensitivity is startling from hands rough
as a gargoyle's face. They gently sweep past
my ears while mine remain folded in my lap—

corpselike and neat. A photograph: young barber
with wife wrapped in postwar bliss, azure future
stretched out like a whisper, and all I can think
is that one day none of this will be memory?

Chapped hands hovering like leaves in a breeze,
not even so much as a rustle in the crawlspace.
Flecks of hair fall, scissors scratch light,
mottled linoleum an autumn grave waiting

to be swept. How easy to imagine that photograph
tucked away like a handkerchief in his burial garb.
The one who hangs on the longest dies twice.

FORM

Sure enough, breaking news,
    a pastor sermonizing Nietzsche
        burst into flame but will not burn.

On another channel a mother in shambles
    sobs damp moons into her sleeve
        over her child who sprouted wings

in the middle of meatloaf dinner—
    last seen occupying the airspace
        over downtown Detroit. Yesterday,

there was a funeral at the edge
    of town and you drove but got lost
        in a maze of farm roads—scarecrows'

sutured eyes lingered on you long after
    you'd given up and gone home. You
        remembered how each of them, stuffed

into a body they didn't choose, resembled
    your own plight, and it made your heart
        sink into your chest like damp linens.

FOR YEARS

my father drifted off to the midnight shift,
a kind of purgatory where he became king
of the trilobites, of silence, of pickle jars
and funeral rites. I'd see him in broad daylight
dozing over the rusty hedge clippers—
dreams like swollen insect bites, dreams
of sweltering leper colonies budding sores
where eyes used to go, blinking sores
that made him shudder awake and look
over at me like a gondolier who just lost his
libretto and gondola on a lousy poker hand.

SURGERY

-for my wife

I. *Notes on the Waiting Room*

Then fluorescent lights tongue the sleepers.
Then the rigged puppet things get stuck

in revolving doors. Then sterile doesn't
have a smell—lymph node, duct work,

broken clavicle, fresh coat of paint
for the all-night benders. *The whites*

are in a row, clattered the nurses.

II. *Letter for Safe Return*

Dear Regina,

> Once they put you under, they'll start
> pulling in other directions like
> your head was fixed to rails. Let
> the stars unfasten and wander
> from their constellations;
> let the luminous things hold and
> guide you; yes, let them go out
> ahead and coax you from the fog.
>
> Swamp trails, tiny buttery rivulets,
> parked cars blistered with rain,
> a pinch of Nicaraguan tobacco.
> These will smell new when you
> come back, rediscovered, mediocre.
> You'll ache again for the cold
> curve of needle under your skin.
> You'll listen harder for the soft
> places between guitar strings
> that used to hide you so well.

The hospital will quiet tonight
to a morphine drip, loose
gowns, loading dock cigarette
breaks, jaundiced newborns,
bedpans, obstetric clamps,
gurneys near the fresh linens,
morgue freezer, little chapel,
loved ones bent in awkward prayer.

REMINISCING SKYROS

Under the couch cushion I find
a tangle of octopuses, olive groves
salting in the wind, Hera grooming
the northern crags and vineyards
from Zeus's beard, a slight drizzle of
Mediterranean blue that could upset
the rest of my afternoon. There goes
a fishing boat; there goes sunlight
dusting the worn path; there goes
my wasted life, my decrepit mule.

HAPPENS SLOWLY

After an hour or so of feeling sorry for myself,
the mutt on the front porch grumbled.

An old lover galloped past like an oversized orgasm
riding an Appaloosa mare, and then all the staplers

of heaven and hell joined ranks to fasten Antony
and Cleopatra to a government-issue cheese wheel

the size of Nebraska. These things happened.
The proof of which can be found anywhere

you like—in the trees the bees are busy building
an army of jelly donuts. Perhaps you should ask them.

Ask the Yellow Pages chocked full of candidates
and astronauts and whistlers of dark and melodious

pinwheels. While you're at it, ask the empty locker
in your stomach for directions to the nearest

24-hour laundromat. I know that pretty soon
you'll catch my drift, and ride it like the billowed

end of some cockamamie parachute all the way
back to the soft, dysfunctional, waiting earth.

ABOUT THE DEAD

At the museum, I stop at a painting: *St. Francis Contemplating a Skull.*
An upturned human skull nestled in his joined hands—

empty sockets contemplating St. Francis. What remains
of the dead fascinates me. In Paris, I wandered

the Catacombs for hours looking at the bones—
stacked so neatly. The plagues were so efficient

at producing bones to stack—the churches' graveyards
dug up and brought by horse-cart under moonlight

to the vacant sarcophagi of the old Roman quarries.
At Père-Lachaise, I witnessed a young couple fucking

on Jim Morrison's grave. They kept it up for nearly
twenty minutes before they were forcibly removed.

The man's cock remained a hard, diligent protester
bouncing as they hauled him away over the cobblestone path

out of the cemetery—something still locked up inside him.

THREE

As Broken in the End

MY BROTHER'S HOUSE

When I came around back, I found him
leaned against the post like a shovel,
hands blistered around an amber
bottle. He'd been hoeing weeds

all day in a garden that long ago
had gone back to God—*Sure did
make a mess of it*, he said. We
walked out to the skiff buried under

long whiskers of grass near the pond.
When we were kids we'd stuff
our bottom lips with tobacco and spit,
gaze out into a field and spit away

hours as though we were old men,
mortgages and busted marriages,
guts rotting out with cancer.
A snapper's head broke the surface.

I knew his wife had left him—he didn't
have to say. I asked for a beer and
he pointed to a cooler next to the house.
I grabbed two. Just then, the dobbers

started to rise from the ground, whirling
like miniature buzzards as a red light
folded over us; for a second, everything
was all right, almost like we'd been saved.

IT'S NO SECRET

People in this airport look miserable,
fed up with the miracle
of manned flight, the rusted
sun, the gigantic tin cans wheeling
across the tarmac. Someone's child

spreads her arms and circles
through the terminal, a buzz
escaping her thin lips as she veers
past a handicapped woman
escorted by a tall man in a blue

vest. I wish I could tell the girl
with pigtails and wings for arms
that we're all secretly waiting
for the moment our bodies unbuckle
from the ground and rise into blue;

but I imagine that, like me, one day
she will find her father gripping
the armrest of the red sofa, eyes
like white marbles cut in half,
scotch melted into water on a coaster.

FLOAT TRIP

One generation has tended to this river the same
as the last and we've come here to mock that.
We've come here to inflate tubes and laze

down a mild stretch on an unseasonably
mild July afternoon. To drink our fill
of the local scenery, to tourist our way

through the giant cave—the only thing
worth remembering besides the vultures
painting their circles across the overcast

sky. You couldn't find Sullivan, MO
on a map. You couldn't imagine people
actually live there but they do—grow old

mowing their one acre of lawn, watching
satellite TV in their one level A-frame.
And what could we offer them besides

the fleeting miracle of our presence
in such a backwoods landscape? We're
students, poets, novelists, actors, animators,

musicians strumming our only note,
weekend philosophers bent on solidifying
our contempt for the local stock whose

imagination carries them back to a leather
sofa in the den and a NASCAR Sunday.
What could we know of people contained

between the shoulders of a rural highway?
We know nothing. We inflate our tubes
before settling onto the river, light cigars

and paddle with one hand. Forgive us,
we've brought you no answers. You who
know this river and a God as tangible as

the white plates you scoop breakfast from.
I apologize for our unwelcome intrusion.
We offer nothing; we take it all in return.

GETTING ARRESTED

I know I'm not the only drunk in the tank,
logging lonely hours on a gurney bunk,
whiskering off a few fingers of scotch—
there goes a poor bastard heaving out
a bluesy riff of vomit, praying to his virgin
mother and all her Tupperware friends.
                                    Sure,
the cops got patience and sobriety,
but I've got a flounce in my pocket, a toenail
chandelier, a diamond man in Calcutta,
an appetite for all things burritoesque.
I can occupy the infinity between now
and bail time with ease. Orange, my favorite
way to color a hillside, is also somewhat
complementary to my personality—
                                    nothing
rhymes with either of us. Chain me down,
throw the dogs at me and unleash the book.
Give my bread to the guy down the hall.
We've got all night to start choosing sides.

TOO MANY HILLSIDES FOR THE DEAD

How long will we continue to fill them
with fathers and mothers and for what?

They may as well be monuments to wind,
soil, grass, trees, an empty bucket

slowly filled over the course of the summer
with rainwater. Our dead just float there

in those lidded ferryboats—most
stopped twiddling their thumbs long ago

having remembered all there is to glean
from a life like any other; and now,

they lean against the wood frames
like turnips wondering why nobody

ever comes to visit, why such lovely
vistas go on unnoticed by the living.

GLASS OF WATER

The trick is to turn the glass
and its content, contaminant,
ukulele in a sock drawer, alimony,
overgrown field across the street,
loose gown in an age of tightening,
fists like steel hammers, art made
from whatever's handy: glass
of water, browning apple heart,
unruly goldenrod in an age
of bolting things down faster than
a flock of Norwegian base jumpers,
salmon vaulting the slipstream
while a silver bullet shatters the dead
harmonica like a note, fathomless
okra coughed up in handkerchiefs
made from ordinary glass and
water in a world where even
the cheap seats cost your firstborn,
where even the dead rise for buglers
sugarcoating the sun, grapefruiting
the cosmos, water tasting like
a French woman's accent inside
the crowded tunnel, half-moon
catapulting through space in an age
of duct tape and corn flakes and
wisdom like softball-sized hail
in a field of broken glass, water
diving over Norwegian cliffs,
parachute made of water and glass,
atoms malleable at this temperature,
Adams cruising low riders with Eves
in a world, in a world, in a world that,
in the end, was only a container of
water, bathtub sloshing as you slid
in front of me, Whitman loafing
in a field littered with glass hearts,
goldenrod, the outlaw in an age

of vacuum-sealed leftovers and
water at room temperature in a glass:
the trick is to build the Sphinx
from anything but sand and rock,
from anything but the strident wind,
all of the glorious world in a glass,
all of the glorious world in a glass.

NEWS OF SURGERY

A birch limb splintered in the night.
Henry stepped onto the porch
underneath the soffit's awning,

felt his mind try to right itself
like a windsock. It couldn't help
but be Tuesday morning. Before bed,

the doctor had called—surgery
for the cubital tunnel in her elbow.
Henry fell quiet and drifted back

to the merry-go-round in Louisville:
she turned into a dragon and he
the knight, lagging behind. Ahead of them,

a Mexican woman cajoled
a dozen children into a chariot.
We have options, she said.

We always have options, Henry said.
Coffee warmed in the pot.
Henry poured a cup and stirred in

honey and cream. Not even nine o'clock,
and the sky on the windows floated heavier
than a bathtub full of paperweights.

O CAPTAIN! MY CAPTAIN!

So I married the daughter of a police captain.
          It was a lot like marrying into the mob, except
not. I'm sure at times his dreams contained

little paper targets of me, shadows he kept
          hidden during holiday dinners—breaking
bread next to a man with such a penchant

for blatant mischief must've been alarming.
          Background check like a novel. One flagrant
violation of order and decency after another.

Yet, sooner or later, he realized I was just a man.
          Made from the same clay. And it didn't matter
that I played a loose hand, or that my plans

for the future felt more like a rough outline.
          His daughter was pleased. I'd paid every fine.

OPEN MIC

That poor son of a bitch was reading the worst piece
of fiction and now I can scarcely remember anything
from the story but *fish tacos*. I kept thinking

of driving through southern Georgia, billboards
oozing hot boiled peanuts and fetuses and lawyers
and we were listening to actors read Faulkner

on tape. I wished we could all be flushed away
from this earth easy as a dream and the cotton making
every day and the cotton making every day and so

what if the sunset's orangey lips pucker up to fetus
and road kill and fish tacos and Faulkner with the same
belabored nuance as yesterday? Don't even bother

arguing that it dims to anything but more light
followed by light in training followed by a duffle
of sorrow buried under the sweet gum's heavy bough

and a sad dream escaping the chest cavity and my father
in his coveralls glancing over his shoulder—the street
lamp overhead striking its match against the concrete.

It's good, you think, to feel those old synapses
hustling to get in line for roll call
as your mother-in-law clears the table
and offers another beer. *Has anyone*
seen Hirohito, Steeplechase, Polio, the Warsaw Pact?
An aging battalion whistled back
from an almost permanent shore leave,
everyone heavy around the midsection;
only half of the state capitals even bothered
to show up and none of the Oscar winners
from 1965–1985. Then, before you know it,
Alan Shepard is rocketed back onto the moon
driving golf balls into the horizon—
How many of them landed in a bunker?—Australopithecus
holds up two fingers, shrugs, and sinks
back into the fold. You can hear Bessie Smith
warming up with Guns N' Roses, while Rome
and Carthage are reenacting the Punic Wars.
What's the world's largest political party?
What's a marsupial's marsupium better known as?
How many of every ten cats will survive a six-story fall?
Nine Chinese communist pouches to be exact,
shouts the Aegean Sea. By now, you're throwing
bull's-eyes blindfolded and things are getting interesting.
Tammy Faye Baker's tattooed eyebrows are learning
to play a five-string banjo while the War of 1812
French-kisses Jupiter, and Margaret Thatcher
poses for the cover of *Sports Illustrated*. Sure,
you could try and put a stop to it, send everyone
slogging away like melancholic whores, useless,
half-remembered, but you still haven't decided
which one has the most chromosomes—a turkey, a hermit crab
or a human? And wouldn't you like to know.

QUESTIONS OF HEAVEN AND HELL ON SUNSET BLVD

How long did Nietzsche swim upon
that lake of fire before he sank stone

heavy, and how many angels can can-
can atop an upright piano? If fear alone

is the enemy of virtue, who then carries
blankets to the homeless in the park

we pass on our way to lunch this very
afternoon? The Brazilian dish is marked

by beans and rice and some type of meat.
For us, today, that meat is chicken.

Between bites we consider the neon heat
of *Live Nudes* across Sunset Blvd, taking

note of the particular varieties of human
indulgence, the possible colors in heaven.

RICK AND THE HOOKER

Fuck this shit, Rick said as he inched
up the peak of the three-story condo,
Bossman doesn't pay me enough.

I was nineteen, working for gas money,
and I held his cutpot all day while he
dipped and brushed and coated fascia

boards a bright white veneer semigloss.
Over lunch break he told me a story
about his hooker sucking him off

in a motel room the night before—*she
hit the pipe and blew it into my cock.
I was hard as a diamond for four hours.*

I couldn't make this shit up. I couldn't
make up his slack face worn out from
too many weeks at seven dollars an hour,

just enough at week's end to cover
the motel bill and another night
with Angel. Thankfully, Rick didn't wait

for me to chime in with some anecdote.
We painted out the rest of the day
as though nothing particular had happened.

I WATCHED HER GOING INTO A GAS STATION,

hips rocking like a pendulum—hips with a purpose.
She walked like most people wish they could fuck.
Spark blonde hair streaked with store-bought low-lights
dropping down between her shoulder blades.
Six splendid inches of midriff. A delivery man
stacking beer onto a dolly lost his focus,
a nervous engine backfired, and a case
of Keystone crashed across the concrete.

A minute later she came out the swinging doors
cuffing two packs of Camels, and slipped on the back
of an Indian Kneeslider with a chrome, four-foot rooster-tail,
custom-painted skull-and-bones gas tank,
and a set of psycho chubby ape handlebars.
The kid gripping the throttle was about eighteen,
probably a dropout working down at his uncle's garage.
He wore black leather in August. The deep-throated

engine fired up an avalanche of noise.
Watching the two of them made me and everyone else there
feel that much older, our lives and Toyota Tercels
that much more pointless. They drifted out of the station
and roared. I screwed on the gas cap and shuffled toward
the swinging doors, an ear cocked to the highway,
waiting for them to disappear.

AS BROKEN IN THE END

It wasn't June but late August when
my father slowed the minivan

onto the shoulder—a sign: *Hot
Boiled Peanuts*, a white paper bag

turning translucent with grease,
oil cooling on the steering wheel.

What brand of wisdom does one buy
from a roadside stand swaddled

in Spanish moss at the tail end
of a Floridian summer on the last

family vacation? Not a single word
was ever spoken about what it meant

to quietly raise a family, to suffer
as his father suffered, to be a man.

YEA, WE WEPT, WHEN WE REMEMBERED ZION

The chaplain was apologetic. "I'm sorry, sir, but just about all the prayers
I know are rather somber in tone and make at least some passing reference to
God."
"Then let's get some new ones."

-Joseph Heller
Catch 22

In this world of rivers and oceans old
and deep, of land blackened from spent fires
left by travelers who've long since moved to the city
and found a kind of love dewing the morning
commute; inside the basin of Los Angeles

is another basin, and inside that one, another,
deeper and sandier than the one before.

From this lowest basin, I pray for a southern
swell to gently rock the coastal waters
of Malibu, to produce waves fit for kings.
That we may brave midday traffic past the 405.
That I may lilt on my surfboard in the chilly,

springtime Pacific, waiting for a hand
to move me ashore. Before this world

there was another, and before that one,
another—like one of those Russian dolls
I bought in Moscow last winter and placed
on the mantle; a conversation piece. I pray
for more conversation pieces and more

conversations about such pieces in rooms framed
with mahogany clear-cut from an extinct forest.

Extinction is such a harsh word. I pray for words
that soften with each use until we may forget
their meaning altogether. I pray to never
become extinct or fashionable. I pray to live
inside the hallowed walls of your mouth forever.

ONLY THEN

The Hemingway Short Story
is a stubby, torpedo shaped cigar
that responds well to fire. It lasts
in the way we last: smoke
of our body becoming air,
becoming breeze, becoming
the cold front that slams its thick
skull against a tree, against a forest,
against the town, where as a boy,
I slept with a brown teddy bear
—threadbare buttons in
its grooved sockets—that bear
had seen it all come and go
and knew the familiar sting
of quarrelsome parents lighting
the hallway, had often buried
itself in the backyard under
the silver maple: a makeshift
graveyard where the sun
fell to its knees, the winsome
sun pressing a shadow against
another grave. I left flowers.
My father would light those
stubby brown cigars and lean
over the rail of the back deck
like a Buddhist shaving his head
in the dark; he would smoke and
stare past the forest and imagine
the coming winter and the next
and before long his parturient
gaze fell back upon the house,
and I could smell the rush
of spent tobacco as he brushed
past. I can smell it now. We
don't talk about such things
in polite conversation although
I wish we could. Then I could

show you the night a tree fell
on our house, the truculent
wind escaping the forest's lungs,
the lightning bluing our crushed
wooden deck, my mother's ruffled
blackwatch nightgown, felled tree
snug against the roof, a hundred years
of growing towards this scene.

ACKNOWLEDGMENTS

A special thanks to the editors of the following publications where some of these poems first appeared (some in slightly different versions):

American Literary Review:	"It's No Secret"
Another Chicago Magazine:	"Glass of Water"
Antioch Review:	"Variations on a Political Theme"
Bellevue Literary Review:	"As Broken in the End"
Concelebratory Shoehorn Review:	"At Church," "Passport," "Preparing the Table," and "Still-Life Minus Fruit"
Connecticut Review:	"Too Many Hillsides for the Dead"
Cream City Review:	"Happens Slowly"
Cutthroat:	"Float Trip" and "News of Surgery"
Dark Horse:	"Red Roof Inn"
Exit 7:	"Peregrination" and "Open Mic"
Fourth River:	"I'm Explaining a Few Things," "Creating the Garden," "Box," and "Reminiscing Skyros"
Harpur Palate:	"I watched her going into a gas station,"
Hunger Mountain:	"Alice"
Moon City Review:	"Surgery"
New York Quarterly:	"Henry's Blues," "An Apology," and "For Years"
North American Review:	"The Dead Cause"
Passages North:	"Funhouse of Mirth"
Rattle:	"Crossing the Gap"
RHINO:	"About the Dead" and "Form"
roger:	"Saxifrage"
Saint Ann's Review:	"Outside Pinckneyville" and "Wheat Field with Crows"
Southeast Review:	"Yea, we wept, when we remembered Zion"
Southern Humanities Review:	"Decampment" and "Inside the Skull"
Sou'wester:	"O Captain! My Captain!"

Subtropics:	"Getting Arrested" and "Trivial Pursuit"
Tampa Review:	"The Second Coming of Christ in the Form of a North American Alligator"
The Smoking Poet:	"Only Then"
Valparaiso Poetry Review:	"My Brother's House"

"Decampment" (appearing in Vol. 44.1 of the *Southern Humanities Review*) has been adapted to screen by Josh Mossotti as an animated short film (www. decampment.com).

"The Dead Cause" was awarded the 2009 *North American Review's* James Hearst Poetry Prize by contest judge Robert Pinsky, and "Getting Arrested" was awarded an Academy of American Poets Prize by contest judge Robert Wrigley. "Inside the Skull" was awarded Honorable Mention for the 2009 *River Styx* International Poetry Prize by contest judge Stephen Dunn.

An audio version of the poem "Crossing the Gap" is available on *Rattle's* official website.

"I watched her going into a gas station," was awarded first place in the 2008 Roxana Rivera Memorial Poetry Prize by contest judge Sandy Longhorn. It appeared in a limited edition contest chapbook. An audio version of the poem is available on *Harpur Palate's* official website.

"Only Then" was featured in the December 2009 Cigar Lounge section of *The Smoking Poet*, an online literary journal that blends the love of literature with fine cigars. "At Church," "Passport," "Preparing the Table," and "Still-Life Minus Fruit" were featured in the online April 2011 issue of *Concelebratory Shoehorn Review.*

Particular gratitude goes out to Rodney Jones and everyone else who helped with this manuscript: Jenna Bazzell, Mark J. Brewin, Edward Brunner, David Clewell, Allison Joseph, Adrian Matejka, Lindsay Mossotti, Hannah New, Erin Quick, and Amie Whittemore. I am grateful to Michael Spooner, Dan Miller and everyone else at Utah State University Press for bringing this book to publication, and I am also indebted to the various contest judges— Sandy Longhorn, Robert Pinsky, Robert Wrigley, and of course Garrison Keillor—whose decisions have meant a great deal to me personally.

Finally, a very special thanks goes to Kerry James Evans whose friendship, insight and knowledge has been indispensable; to Josh, my brother, for creating the art for this book and for providing a wellspring of inspiration via our workshops together—the surfing, cigars and scotch, his unrivaled artistic talent; and of course, to my wife Regina for her love, her confidence and her reservoirs of patience (not to mention her cold reads which have tested the mustard of every poem in here).

I'd also like to thank my entire family for their help and understanding— without which, none of this would have been possible.

ABOUT THE AUTHOR

Travis Mossotti received a BA in English and French from Webster University and an MFA in poetry from Southern Illinois University—Carbondale. Recently a faculty lecturer at the University of California—Santa Cruz, his poetry appears widely in literary journals, including *American Literary Review, Antioch Review, Bellevue Liteary Review, Cincinnati Review, Harpur Palate, Poetry Ireland Review, Rattle, Southern Humanities Review, Subtropics* and many others. Mossotti was awarded the James Hearst Poetry Prize from the *North American Review* in 2009, and "Decampment," the opening poem to *About the Dead*, was adapted to screen in 2010 as an animated short film (www.decampment.com). Mossotti currently resides in St. Louis with his wife, Regina.

THE MAY SWENSON POETRY AWARD

The annual award in her name honors May Swenson as one of America's most provocative and vital writers. In John Hollander's words, she was "one of our few unquestionably major poets." During her long career, May was loved and praised by writers from virtually every major school of American poetry. She left a legacy of nearly fifty years of writing when she died in 1989. She is buried in Logan, Utah, her birthplace and hometown.